I0845046

# Finding Nature's Magic

*Janet G. Nestor*

# Finding Nature's Magic

Janet G. Nestor

**Published June 2020**



**Typesetting:** Frances Phelps

**Cover Design:** Frances Phelps

**Final edit:** Theresa Thompson

**ISBN:** 979-8-65067-855-7

*Dedication*

To all the evolvers, the doers

To the preservers, and the growers

To unity, awareness, and conscious living

To Mother Earth who makes all of our lives possible.

# CHAPTER I

# Introduction

*As children, we are very sensitive to nature's beauty, finding
miracles and interesting things everywhere. As we grow up,
we tend to forget how beautiful and magnificent the world is.
There is magic and wonder for eyes who know how to look with
curiosity and love.*

*—Ansel Adams*

We have all had special, heartfelt experiences while enjoying nature. Often, we've been afraid to share our extraordinary moments because they seem so far out of the norm. Maybe you've heard the sounds of the trees, felt the energy of the moon, or seen a fairy flit through your flower garden. I know that I've kept many of my stories personal, sharing only with a few people who I thought might understand.

The truth is that our nature experiences are not abnormal or rare. Our experiences are normal and natural, and these mystical moments are our teachers. We are part of nature and we share all that we are with her every day. And she shares all she is with us every day of our lives.

Some of the stories in this eBook may stretch your understanding of the truth. However, the stories are true, and I can assure you that many others have written about similar events in their lives. As we evolve, Mother Nature allows us to understand and experience more of her truths.

# CHAPTER II

# The Color of Leaves

*I'm so glad I live in a world where there are Octobers.*

*—Lucy Maud Montgomery*

In the spring, Earth comes to life in green, decorated with flowers and blooming trees. Months later, fall brings colors fit for an artist's canvas as the trees shine their colors for all of us to enjoy. Each season has its own magnificence.

Do you know why the leaves turn from green to yellow, orange, red, and brown?

The warm days and the cool nights help determine the colors we enjoy. Just like you and I have a biological chemistry that maintains our body's functioning, the trees have a chemistry that protects them and their way of life.

Trees have a yearly cycle. During the summer, the green chlorophyll dominates the color of the leaves. Chlorophyll, a biochemical, covers up the yellow and orange colors that are always present. Think of the chlorophyll as a blanket that hides the fall colors until the light from the sun is less bright and the nights are cooler.

The red color is not present in the summer months, yet during the fall, the red color helps the tree prepare for the spring season when the leaves will bud again. The red color comes from anthocyanins, a chemical that is produced in cool, dry weather. The anthocyanins are the result of glucose that gets trapped in the leaves. During the summer, the light of the sun breaks down the glucose. When the sun is too cool to break down the glucose, we are blessed with the magnificent red- and purple-colored leaves of the fall

I feel very fortunate to have lived in six different states across the United States. Each is spectacular in unique ways. But for me, nothing beats the mountains of North Carolina, Virginia, and West Virginia in the fall.  If you have a weekend free for travel, I recommend you grab a camera and fill your heart and eyes with the spectacular beauty of the colorful autumn landscape.

# CHAPTER III

# Tree Beings

*Trees exhale for us so that we can inhale them to stay alive. Can we ever forget that? Let us love trees with every breathe we take until we perish.*

*—Munia Khan*

Approximately twenty years ago, a small forest changed my life. As I walked along the greenway at the edge of my neighborhood, I noticed a man standing in the woods that separated the walkway from the highway. I stopped to watch the man. He stared at me and lifted his arms as if to say, "Lady, I'm just doing my job." He bent down and began to cut down the first tree in the small forest of maybe one hundred trees. The saw was loud in the quiet of early morning, and what happened next was a trauma not only for the trees and the land, but for me.

An audible call went up among the trees. The sound was bone-chilling and was a vibrational scream, and a warning that something bad was about to happen. The sound went through the little forest tree by tree until it was a song of terror. I realized I was watching the beginning of a mass murder. The trees "knew" they were going to die. They were just as terrified as you and I would be if we knew our life was about to end violently. My eyes are brimming with tears remembering the fear of those trees.

I couldn't stop what was happening. However, I turned around, walked home, and wrote an editorial that was published in the city newspaper. Only one person responded. Nevertheless, our neighborhood came together to protest the planned development. Instead of new homes, the land is now a small park and part of the greenway.

Today, I view trees as fellow beings with emotions, a level of conscious awareness, and the ability to send messages to friends and family.  Research has proven that trees do communicate with each other, can make sounds, have a heartbeat, and live in family groups.

It is time for human beings to wake up to the truth — to understand that when we cut down a tree, we end an important part of life on this planet. It is time to realize that damaged land takes a long time to heal, function, and provide the necessities of life for the other beings who live among the trees, and in the earth.

# CHAPTER IV

# Beyond What I Thought was Truth

*Whoever has learned how to listen to trees no longer wants to be a tree. He wants to be nothing except what he is. That is home. That is happiness.*

**—Herman Hesse**

When we lived in California, I purchased a small ficus tree. At the time, she was about two feet tall. She was healthy and strong and thrived in our home.

After three years, we moved back to the East Coast. The ficus tree moved with our family. She was a little bigger now and lived in our family room where there was a lot of light. She survived the week in a moving van and continued to thrive, something unusual for this kind of indoor tree.

She moved again from Virginia to North Carolina. This time she wasn't too happy about the move and became ill. By this point, our relationship was strong, and she was a long-time member of our family. I'd read the book, The Secret Life of Plants and decided to try to communicate with her. First, I put my open palm under a branch. I practiced energy medicine, so I thought she might respond to the energy and feel better. I don't know about feeling better, but I began to notice a gentle moving of the branch in response to my hand. I was thrilled. It wasn't much, but it was movement. I asked two friends to confirm the movement to make sure my imagination was not running wild.

I was giving my ficus friend plant food. I poured the food into her pot one day, and I heard her voice say, "Are you trying to kill me?" Obviously, I was not. I took a leap of faith and asked her what she needed to get well. She gave me the exact ratio of nutrients she needed to survive. I couldn't find a plant food that met her specifications. I bought two different kinds of food, both having some of the requirements she'd specified. I gave her the first food. She didn't like it. I gave her the second food. It was not what she wanted or needed. Finally, I purchased an inexpensive plant food from a hardware store, put a few drops of it in water and gave her the food. She said clearly, "This is not perfect, but it will do." By this time her branches were almost bare, but they began to bud new leaves. Before long, she was fully leaved and healthy again.  My view of life was continuing to grow and change. My plant was consciously communicating with me and was able to interact with my mind to tell me what she needed.

After nine years, it was time to move again. The ficus tree had been a part of our family for twelve years. She went into the moving van and we moved into a new home in a new city. This time her home was in my upstairs office. She was huge now and at six feet with long beautiful branches, she needed a wide-open space. But she was unhappy with her home. We tried the medicine again and this time nothing worked. Gradually over a couple of years, she slowly passed away, in part from loneliness. It was the first time she had not lived in the heart of the family. Spending time with me a couple of hours a day was not enough time to satisfy her needs.

Talk to your house plants and the plants growing in your yard. They love your voice. Play music for your plants. They love music. They are Plant Beings. Just like trees, they are able to respond to you and form a relationship with you as their caregiver.

There is only one circle of life. You and I as human beings are just one part of the circle. We are part of nature. We are one species out of many species of life on this planet. Each species is important, and each species has something to offer the world.

# CHAPTER V

# The Morning Glory Miracle

*I think plants present an opportunity for people to look closely at something and get invested in something that's truly very much outside of themselves.*

## —Hope Jahren

Once in a while, something happens that has no explanation. You see it, examine it, ask questions about it, and discuss it with friends and family. Even while asking questions, you know there is no logical answer. You know you are experiencing one of nature's miracles. You know what you are witnessing is a synchronicity meant to raise your awareness.

Here is the short story of the Morning Glory Mystery. The miracle happened about four years ago when my temporary home was a second story condo.

My downstairs neighbor planted morning glories each summer. They grew up the deck pole and formed a beautiful green vine with blooms that made my deck rail come alive. One day, she pulled the plants from the ground and cut the vine away from her patio pole. This left the remaining plant crawling beautifully around my deck rail without roots. There was an immediate wilting of some of the vines, but most of the them continued to live, grow, bud, and bloom. I had no idea the mother plant had been pulled from the ground! I thought the cooler weather was causing them to wilt a little bit.

At least ten days went by, and yet each day there were more and more blooms. As each day passed, I was more and more determined to share this fantastic story. The vine was covered in buds and new growth. It was almost spooky. The magical morning glory was a deafening testament to the will to live! I did not touch the vine as I was so amazed by its stamina. I knew it was being cared for by an unseen force — the same unseen force that takes care of you and me.

So, what is your perspective? Do you have the same will to live regardless of impossible circumstances? Do I? I think when our life support is cut off, we expect to die. This plant did not expect to die. This morning glory was determined to not only live, but to thrive.

This humble morning glory plant is a mind-awakening visual af-firmation that validates what I've been teaching for years. Within you — and every living being — is everything you need to thrive! If it is in this morning glory, then it is within you and me.

The powerful plant used every bit of strength it had to burst forth with the most beautiful blooms of the season — to create a vine full of buds that were determined to burst into glorious beauty. This rootless plant lived at least three weeks without a source of water or food. All she had was the moisture from the air, and the warmth of an autumn sun to sustain her.

This morning glory miracle vine is a gift meant to teach a very valuable lesson. You and I can become more of our authentic, dynamic selves. We can trust without question. We can believe that there is a power beyond our mind and body that is all-knowing and pure love. We know that real support is there for us when everyone is telling us there is no hope.

*Morning glories on second-level balcony*

# CHAPTER VI

# Nature's Angels

*Faeries, come take me out of the dull world,*
*For I would ride with you upon the wind,*
*Run on the top of the disheveled tide,*
*And dance upon the mountains like a flame.*

**—William Butler Yeats**

I have not always believed that little fairy beings exist. My interest escalated when Elizabeth Kubler-Ross, the woman famous for writing about grief, death, and dying, wrote in her last book that she'd enjoyed entertaining fairies in her garden. That was it! If this medical doctor and researcher was seeing fairies in her garden, then I wanted to see them too.

A trusted friend sent a photo of a wilting daisy in a vase with a little fairy hovering over it in a tender, protective way. There was no Photoshop in this photo! I have another friend who sees fairies in her backyard flower garden and has photos to prove it. Knowing the little ones are real, I was eager to meet the fairy beings that live in my yard.

My book, *Yeshua: One Hundred Meaningful Messages* was written during the summer of 2014. I was doing special energetic exercises at bedtime and in the morning before getting up and my sensory system was wide open. My openness allowed me to hear Yeshua's voice in my mind and write down the words he spoke as he spoke them.  One day after a writing session, I sat down on the couch in front of a wall of windows to gaze at nature and rest. It was then that the fun began.

A tiny almost transparent ball of energy flitted across the windows, then turned back shocked that I'd seen her. Once she realized I could see her, she decided to play hide-and-seek. She flew to the middle of the window, stayed there, and then darted out of my view. She'd fly to the edge of the glass and peek at me. I imagined her laughing. We played like this for about 20 minutes and I giggled with excitement the entire time. She was having fun darting about while I watched in pure delight.

I sat quietly so I would not frighten my new little friend. I just watched, giggled, and whispered, "Hello sweetie." I didn't see her again for the rest of the summer. A year or so passed without a fairy sighting. Then one day, I saw that same little blue sparkling ball of energy dart across the width of my old pine tree and disappear into the green area to the left of the path. Just knowing she is still close by brings me great joy.

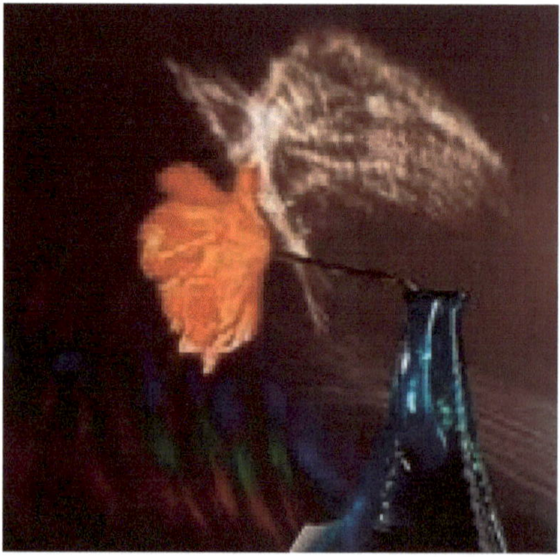

*Photo credit: Dr. Barbara Stone, www.souldetective.net*

# CHAPTER VII

# Mothering the Mason Bees

*The keeping of bees is like the direction of sunbeams.*

**—Henry David Thoreau**

A group of mason bees came to live at my house one spring. They are wonderful little bees because they don't sting, and they are great pollinators. I hope to entice you to invite these bees into your flower garden next spring. I've decided I want three mason bee houses instead of one!

My daughters purchased the first bee house and a little box of bees that hatched before I could introduce them to their new home. All but two flew off never to be seen again. However, the last time I checked, 12 momma bees had laid eggs and sealed them into a little cylinder nursery. The exciting thing is that the bees keep watch and make repairs as needed. The bee eggs will hatch in the spring after the weather is warm. Supposedly, the bees who hatch from my bee house will return for the next season.

When you look at the photo of the bee house, you'll see there are two kinds of nests. There are traditional nests with yellow clay seals, but the majority of the bees made and sealed their little nurseries with bits of grass. I watched several of the nurseries being built. The momma bee works very hard to keep her eggs safe until they hatch in the spring. The mud doors seemed to be partially washed away with a hard rainfall. The bees reseal the door by patching the whole with new mud, creating safety for the eggs inside.  I was shocked when I first noticed their repair work. Bees are flat out amazing little beings.

*Mason bee house*

You can buy mason bees and their houses from Amazon or specialty mason bee websites. I have to say the bees are addictive. I check on them every day when I am at home. I love watching for new mason bee nurseries and enjoy watching the momma bees build their nest.

I'm going to plant three butterfly bushes for the bees and their butterfly friends. The bees love my sage plants and their red blooms. They enjoyed lantanas and every tree that blooms during the summer. Bees love the fig tree, so I hung the first house on a safe inner branch. However, the bees needed more sun and did not begin to populate their house until I moved it to a sunny area.

I feel like a bee mother. I'm protective and hoping for a lot of bee births in the spring, and a new batch of eggs to mother until they hatch.

Mason bee houses are inexpensive, and since these bees don't sting, they are safe for children and anyone allergic to bee stings. Think about adding one or two in your yard. It is an educational experience and every bee house and bee helps to create a healthier living environment for everyone.

*Mason bees capping their tunnels*

# CHAPTER VIII

# Mr. and Mrs. Cardinal

*Somewhere a bird sang, its chant hanging plaintive and melancholy in the still air...I think it's a sort of lark or something. Our tradition has it that they sing with the voices of lost lovers. If the stars are smiling on them, you will hear its mate call back in a moment.*

**—Jane Johnson**

Two summers ago, I noticed that the little woods next to my house was home to a cardinal family. Mom and Dad Cardinal were so much in love. Each morning, he would sing to her from a tree in the wooded area behind our house, and she would answer. It was such a beautiful sound. I came to look forward to and cherish their songs.

Then Hurricane Florence came to visit the coast. To my surprise, the couple made it through Florence and were there to greet me when we were able to return home. Then Hurricane Michael came to visit our area. The winds were blowing, and the trees were tested by the winds. I was looking out of my office window, and I saw my cherished red friends sitting in a small tree that was being whipped around like it was a twig.

I wanted to go out and grab them out of the tree, yet I realized that without a ladder I'd never be able to reach them. And, would they allow me to carry them to safety? When the wind picked up speed, she was the first to lose her grip. She disappeared without a sound. I continued to watch. Each time a strong gust of wind came, Mr. Cardinal would scream as the wind whipped the limb back and almost to the ground. He held on through three gusts of wind. On the fourth gust, he screamed and disappeared into the woods. I ran outside and into the woods to look for them, but they were nowhere to be found.

After the storm was over, I searched for the cardinals again and waited patiently to see if they would return. After a bit of time, he returned alone. I swear that he came to let me know he was okay. He sat in the tree beside the house and sang his love song. It was heartbreaking because there was no response.

When he left that day, he did not return. The next spring, he came to the old nesting place and began to sing. No one was answering him for the longest time. Then one day, I heard a reply from a distance. He continued to sing, and she continued to reply. This went on for days.

Somewhere in the woods, there was a wedding. This time, the singing was not as loud or as joyful, but he'd found a partner.

Right now, I'm in an apartment in another city and guess who showed up in the tree outside our living room window — the new Mr. and Mrs. Cardinal. They sang their songs one morning about a week ago, flew off, and I've not heard from them again.

Was it a different cardinal couple? I don't think so. I think we've become friends.

# CHAPTER IX

# Folk Medicine: Remedies From Nature

*When plant leaves are turning brown you don't paint the leaves green. You look at the causes of the problem. If only we treated our bodies the same way.*

**—Dr. Frank Lipman**

How do you keep healthy on a budget? You live on a farm where all your food is organic. Most of it is fresh off the tree or vine, you eat fresh eggs from the hen house, and you get lots of good exercise. I lived on a farm as a child. I no longer live there, but I honor the experience. It was there that I learned to love Mother Nature and respect the natural approach to health.

Here are some home remedies from my childhood and Mother Nature:

1. Dandelion tea from roots dug up from the yard and boiled in the kitchen. Dandelion tea helps you detox your body.

2.  A sassafras tree in the yard makes it easy to chew the leaves
    and the stems to help with digestion

3.  Ginseng roots from the forest

4.  Onion plasters for chest congestion

5.  Mustard plasters for chest congestion

6.  Mint leaves for a sour stomach

7.  Gargling saltwater for a sore throat

8.  Spoons full of fresh honey to stay healthy. A little honey in a
    cup of hot tea is great for a sore throat

9.  Whole cloves for toothaches and fresh breath

Today, I no longer use a mustard plaster for a cold, but I do drink
dandelion tea almost every day to detox my body. I chew fresh mint
leaves for digestion, or drink water infused with a couple drops of
peppermint oil. I take ginseng supplements for mental stimulation
and overall immune system strength. I'm a believer in local honey
to help with allergies and colds during the winter.

Today, we are reluctant to use these home remedies, but they do work,
and they help minimize the use of over-the-counter medications and
prescription drugs. They help your body heal itself — something we
don't value enough in our modern world of pills and procedures.

I'm sharing a photo of a sassafras tree leaf. The huge sassafras tree
in my great grandmother's yard is one of my happy childhood
memories. Just pull the leaf off the tree and chew! The leaf tastes
good, has no sugar to worry about, and it is fun!

Annie's Remedies is a nice site that explains over 400 herbal uses.

Take a look: https://www.anniesremedy.com/index.php

*Sassafras tree leaf*

# CHAPTER X

# Water: Nature's Miracle

*Water does not resist. Water flows. When you plunge your hand into it, all you feel is a caress. Water is not a solid wall, it will not stop you. But water always goes where it wants to go, and nothing in the end can stand against it.*

*Water is patient. Dripping water wears away a stone. Remember that, my child. Remember you are half water. If you can't go through an obstacle, go around it. Water does.*

## —Margaret Atwood

I learned early in life that living close to the water was a soul gift. There is magic in flowing water. Water is the lifeblood of the Earth, and without it, our planet would be barren.

Water is your lifeblood. Not the red blood that flows through your veins, but the nourishment that helps your body stay in energetic balance. In fact, it is almost impossible for you to be energetically balanced when you are dehydrated. Water is life.

The oceans and the mountains provide negative ions that create relaxation and positive energy. The positive benefits of negative ions are staggering. Not only do they clean the air we breathe, they may also create a biochemical reaction that creates serotonin, the neurochemical that prevents depression.

When you bring negative ions inside your home in the form of Himalayan salt lamps, you create a healthier, relaxed living environment. Negative ions also help you sleep more soundly. The lamps are made of ancient crystalized seawater, and the warmth created by the light bulb causes the lamp to release the feel good ions.

The closer your drinking water is to nature, the better. Water that is bottled, and water that flows from our faucet is dead water. It has been purified chemically, run through machinery and pipes, or bottled up for sale. By the time it gets to you, it needs to be reminded of who it is. You can purchase water bottles that have crystals in them, but even better you can pick up a rock or two from a riverbed, or a rock washed ashore from the ocean waves, clean them, and drop them into a pitcher of water. After a little while, that water becomes more alive and healthier to drink. My friend, a biologist, turned me onto this trick several years ago. If you purchase five-gallon water jugs, you can even place stones or crystals on the flat top of the jug. It is amazing, and you will see a positive difference in the water when you drink it. Your body will thank you.

You can use water to elevate your mood, and reduce your stress. It is easy. Write the word "love" on a piece of paper and tape it to the bottom of a water glass. Clear glass is best. When you drink water from the love-infused water, you improve your immune system and health. If you are trying to relax and feel more positive, you can write "peaceful" on the glass to help you adopt the attitude of peace.

Your body is approximately 75% water, and that water is a powerful medicine for your mind, body, and soul.

# Dancing in the Rain

*Some people walk in the rain, others just get wet.*

## —Roger Miller

Trees fascinate me. They give all of us so much more than the oxygen we breathe. They help us heal our mind, body, and soul by taking our emotional and physical pain.  Go find a pine tree — a big one that you can sit under. Use the tree as a back rest. Close your eyes with the intention of relaxing, and in just a few minutes, you will feel rejuvenated. The tree takes your stress and reprocesses it through the earth. Just remember to say thank you.

Over the years, I've developed a relationship with the trees around my house. For over a year, I said good morning to them every day, and then played a song for them using my eight-note chimes. My trees know they are safe as long as our family owns the land.

On certain days, their energy is visible — or perhaps my awareness is stronger on some days. Their energy shimmers around them. It is an amazing sight, and I feel so grateful to be able to experience their biofield. But what I love the most is watching each tree react to a hard rain. I had no idea that each tree responds to weather in their own unique way. They react according to their personalities, just like you and I do. On this particular day, it had been raining for hours. The ground was soaking wet; the wind was gusting. The trees down by the marsh were surrounded by water. I started watching because of the wind. Some of the trees were standing totally still, while others were shivering in the wind and the rain.  My mind went on alert.  It is impossible for the wind to only blow on one tree. Right?

I was waking up to a reality that I did not know existed. I remember thinking that each of these trees is unique. One looked soaked and droopy, totally miserable and perhaps in pain. Most others were just doing their best to weather the storm. But one little tree, a young tree, was having the time of her life. She was literally dancing in the rain. She looked like a teenager on the dance floor reacting to the beat of the music. Once I noticed, I wondered how I'd missed this truth? How could I not notice that some trees are stoic and suffer in silence, while others visibly show their dismay, and yet another is as happy as a clam to be fluttering in the wind and rain.

This is why a spiritual journey is important. It is so important to develop an awareness of your own physical, emotional, and spiritual reactions to everything that goes on around you.

I urge you to be aware the next time there is a long, hard rain. Watch the life outside — the beings that have no shelter from the elements. Understand that they suffer just as we do. And understand that as aware adults, we have a responsibility to do all we can to ease their suffering. Obviously, you can't bring a forest inside or hand each tree an umbrella. But we can send our love and understanding, and let them know they are valued and loved.

Love really is the answer to almost everything.

# CHAPTER XII

# Humans Are Naturally Part of Nature

*Every particular in nature, a leaf, a drop, a crystal, a moment of time is related to the whole, and partakes of the perfection of the whole.*

## —Ralph Waldo Emerson

It is so easy to forget that the human race is a part of nature. We are warm-blooded mammals just like the bears, cows, dogs, and cats. We have forgotten who we are because we've taken ourselves out of the animal kingdom by thinking of ourselves as the supreme form of life. But all mammals have intuition, instinct, blood, bones, a nervous system, a brain, the ability to remember, communicate, and the ability to feel pain, love, and loss. We all live in families. Our females give birth and have the ability to breastfeed our young. All other forms of life have similar systems and the abilities appropriate for their species. Life is life, and all life is important.

How do we look inside ourselves and understand our roles, and the role of humanity on this planet? How do we get to know who we really are and live authentically? The short answer is we connect to the soul of creation. But how do we do that?

My first spiritual experience occurred when I was very young, and I've never forgotten it. I was placed on a blue blanket under a huge maple tree beside my grandmother's house and left alone. It was a beautiful warm day. The sky was a perfect blue, and the leaves were dancing in the wind. As I gazed upward, I merged with Creation. I was one with all that is. That blissful memory is forever a part of who I am. While as a tiny child, I did not understand the meaning of oneness, I cannot remember a time when I did not understand the importance of love and unity.

As a young mother, I was determined to re-find that divine connection I'd experienced years before. At age 30, I'd experienced resting and breathing meditation, enjoyed the experience of no mind, and was guided to feel into my body during a Reality Therapy Class. I loved the experiences, wanted to learn more, and spirit was nudging me forward. However, I was not living a mindful lifestyle.

Mindful living really means living in the moment and embracing who we are inside and out. We all have the ability to live within an awareness and mind-body-spirit connection that allows us to live in peace with ourselves, with others, with Mother Nature, and all other life on this planet. Living in connection and awareness awakens our empathy, a deeper understanding of our own needs, and the needs of others, including the needs of the Earth.

My experience of connected awareness is not unique, but it is important to share. It is this connection that makes us truly human, fully recognizing our innate divinity. I deeply believe that every human being experiences connected awareness at various times in our life. However, we don't always embrace the experience as what it is. We are made to live this way, and we all have the physiology and spiritual capacity to connect to the wisdom of the universe.

To feel into myself and know my own body and its subtleties is a spiritual experience. When I take the time to look inside myself, I lose contact with my immediate environment and gain contact with my higher self — my inner being, my soul self. In this place, I am very aware of my body, how it feels, and my level of relaxation — yet I am not thinking about it. I feel safe, loved, and cared for. Within the silence is everything that is. All the wisdom of the universe is there. I can talk to my body and get a response. I can communicate with my spiritual angels, guides, and teachers, feel their presence, and learn from them. In this space, there is no worry or anxiety. There is only the connection and the awareness it brings.

I don't remember my meditative experiences for very long after I've reconnected to my outer environment. I have to write down my experiences immediately. My journal content is information from a higher state of consciousness, and it may take many readings before I am able to bring what I have learned into daily practice.

To live naturally is to live in freedom.

# CHAPTER XIII

# Thank You Mother Nature

*Look deep into nature, and then you will understand
everything better.*

## —Albert Einstein

My favorite part of mindful living is the connection it fosters with Mother Nature, which brings awareness of the food we eat, and the prevention of excess waste of food and all other natural resources.

My mindful journey began with tai chi walking. As I practiced this art, I was aware of how my weight was distributed on my right and left foot as I stepped forward. I had to pay attention to the alignment between my hip, knee, and ankle. Tai chi walking was walking in a flow of awareness. I became so enthralled with it that I thought it would be wonderful to use the concepts during my morning walk. I began to walk a bit faster and began a practice of slow walking that felt like a meditation. I thought I'd discovered something new as I had not yet discovered Thich Nhat Hanh, a Vietnamese author, spiritual teacher, and all-around mindfulness genius. He is the father of modern-day walking meditation.

When walking in a slow, meditative way, our awareness of the Earth increases as we kiss the Earth with each step, thanking her for sustaining our life. We become aware of our connection to life, to our body, to other people and animals, of the words we speak, how we treat ourselves and others, and most of all, how we treat Mother Earth, and the gifts she provides us.

Mindfulness increases our level of consciousness. I'm more aware of sunrises, sunsets, the moon, stars, other planets, the air, the water, and the essential needs of every living thing. That includes plants and trees living in forests, parks, and along highways and trees, fruits and vegetables living in yards, gardens and on farms. As we begin to understand the needs of dogs, cats, butterflies, flowers, plants, fruits, vegetables, and trees, our awareness reaches a new level: a level of consciousness.

Becoming a conscious gardener is part of conscious living. When we plant our gardens, we ask the seeds, bulbs, plants, and trees what they need to grow successfully. We meet their needs and then we allow them to tell us where they want to live. As we go to the garden to harvest fruits and vegetables, we ask the vegetables and fruits, "Are you ready to be picked and eaten?" It is amazing that as you ask each tomato, cucumber, or apple, the fruit or vegetable will respond with a yes or no. That answer is not spoken out loud but energetically shared. I often hear the answer in my mind, but as I touch the food with my fingers, I hear the vibrational answer.

When we give our food a choice, fruits and vegetables taste better, and food gives us more pleasure. The same goes for the meat we eat. We ask the cow, the pig, the goat, the lamb, the turkey, the chicken, the fish, "Are you ready to give your life to sustain others?" You will get an answer. When you adopt mindful eating and mindful living, this is how you begin to live. Most of us do not kill our own meat, so the thank you is given at the time of food preparation. This is a life-giving and healing activity for all concerned.

When I fix dinner, I say thank you to the food I prepare. "Thank you, potato, for feeding my family today. Thank you, chicken, for your sacrifice that benefits my family." When we make peace with the food we eat, our digestion is more efficient, and the animals, the fruits and vegetables are more content with their gift. We create peace for all concerned. Every living thing likes to hear thank you.

When we see a beautiful flower growing, we don't pick it. We thank it for its beauty and the pleasure it gives to the world. But if we want to cut flowers to bring into our home, we use the same procedure we use for our food. "Are you ready to come into my home to beautify my environment?" Just like the fruit and veggies, the flower says yes or no. And if we are living mindfully, we respect the response and cut a flower that says yes.

Just a little story to end this conversation. I purchased apples at the grocery store. I chose an apple to eat and I clearly heard, "NO! I don't want to be eaten." The shock of the apple's passion stopped me cold. I put the apple back in the bowl and continued to choose other apples to eat. I wanted to understand this particular apple who was so vocal. So, I asked. The apple had a great reason for not wanting to be eaten. It wanted its seeds to grow into trees instead of being thrown away to die. The apple benefited from being asked, and I did too. Now you are benefitting from its reply. The fresh food we eat is alive. It is our job to be kind to the food we eat. In return, our body benefits more from the nutrition the food brings to us, and the food and I are at peace with each other. And the answer is no, I did not eat the apple that said no.

Thank you, Mother Nature, for all that you teach us, all that you provide for us, and for your patience while we learn to treat you with love and respect.

# CHAPTER XIV

# Nature-Based Healing Exercises

*If gratitude is your mantra and mine, the Earth and all her inhabitants will not only be safe, they will thrive.*

*—Janet G. Nestor*

## Pine Tree Healing Exercise

Pine trees are important in Chinese art and in traditional Chinese medicine because they symbolize good health and long life. Various parts of the pine tree are used in treatment, but in itself, a pine tree is a healer. Pine trees welcome your friendship and will take your emotional-spiritual pain and reprocess it for you.

Here are the directions:

1.  Find a pine tree that you can lean against or sit under with your back against the trunk.

2.  Decide what you want to give to the tree to reprocess for you. You can let go of troubling emotions like sadness, grief, or anger. You can also let go of troubling life issues related to

relationships, work, problems with your children getting their homework completed, or worry about illness.

3.  Once you have the emotion or issue you want to work on, jot down the wording. For example, you'll understand these words: I choose to let go of the sadness I've felt since my father's death. However, your body-mind-spirit will respond more fully to these words: I fully and completely embrace acceptance and peace.

4.  Through imagery, send the emotion (in this case sadness) to the tree for reprocessing. Close your eyes and allow the negative energy to flow to the roots of the tree. Let the sadness go and allow the tree to do the rest.  There is no need to worry about leaving your negativity for others to experience. The tree will reprocess the negativity into positivity, and release it back into the environment.

5.  When you've released the emotion or issue, remember two things:

Check in with your mind, body, emotions, and spirit. What does it feel like to be less stressed or less troubled by difficult emotions? Did you have a specific experience as you gave your challenging emotion to the tree for reprocessing? Did you receive a message from the tree or from the wisdom of Creation?

Remember to say thank you to the tree, the roots, and the Earth.

## *Standing Within a Grove of Trees*

Trees are amazing beings that contribute in many ways to the health and welfare of the Earth and the Earth's inhabitants. Trees are comforting, soothing, and their rooted and grounded presence empowers human beings.

Bring a pocket notepad and pen with you for this exercise.

1.  Find a grove of trees, in a quiet place if possible — perhaps along a greenway, in a park, or on a trail winding through a forest.

2.  Once you've found a grove of trees, touch each tree, and stand close to the tree that you are most attracted to.

3.  As you stand quietly, imagine that you are rooted into the Earth just like a tree. See your roots reaching down to the center of the Earth.

4.  Close your eyes and allow yourself to become part of the environment. Inhale and exhale slowly. Focus on the quiet around you. Focus on the trees and their strength and solidarity. Perhaps stand with your hand resting against your favorite tree so it can share more fully with you and you can more fully receive.

5.  After a minimum of five minutes, jot down your experience using your pocket journal.

6.  Each time you do this exercise, the results will be different. After a while, your relationship with the trees will strengthen and you will begin to understand them and communicate with them and a deeper level.

## *Earthing*

Earthing is a rather new word that advocates maintaining contact with the Earth and her magnetic field. All living beings need the Earth's magnetic field to be healthy, yet humans have almost no contact with her Earth's energy.  For best results, walk on the grass with bare feet. Any contact with the Earth is healing. Get your hands in the dirt when planting flowers, fruits, and vegetables. Lay on the grass and watch the clouds go by. The more contact with the Earth, the better. If the weather does not permit, take a moment and simply bend down and touch the ground with your bare hands.

It is important that we thank the Earth for all she gives to us. She is the mother of life. She needs love. She needs understanding. She needs to be toxin free just like we do. As you walk, say thank you for the solidarity of the Earth under your feet. As you sit enjoying the ocean, say thank you to the beautiful sandy beach that is so vibrant and alive. As you sit on a mountain top, say thank you to the mountain for her majestic heights and strength and for the beautiful vista before you.

Understand that every environment is home to many species of life. Respect the environment and do everything you can to maintain it so that the life it supports can continue to live and thrive. Don't throw gum or sticky substances on the ground to prevent bees, butterflies, and small birds from dying in the stickiness. Don't put toxic products on your gardens and lawns to save the animals and insects from a toxic death.

Conscious living is a process. First, we are mindful. Then we become aware. Once we are aware, we become conscious to our needs and the needs of all forms of life.

The End